HARPER HONAN

Mathew Honan made barackobamaisyournewbicycle.com
in February 2008. A contributing editor at *Wired* magazine,
his writing can also be found in Salon.com, *Mother Jones*,
The New York Sun, and *Popular Science*.

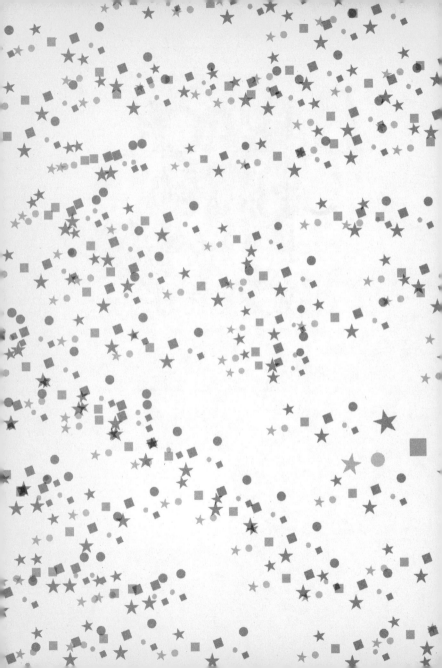

BARACK OBAMA
IS YOUR
NEW BICYCLE

366 Ways He Really Cares

MATHEW HONAN

Illustrated by Omar Lee

GOTHAM
BOOKS

GOTHAM BOOKS
Published by Penguin Group (USA) Inc.
375 Hudson Street, New York, New York 10014, U.S.A.
Penguin Group (Canada), 90 Eglinton Avenue East, Suite 700, Toronto, Ontario
M4P 2Y3, Canada (a division of Pearson Penguin Canada Inc.); Penguin Books Ltd,
80 Strand, London WC2R 0RL, England; Penguin Ireland, 25 St Stephen's Green,
Dublin 2, Ireland (a division of Penguin Books Ltd); Penguin Group (Australia), 250
Camberwell Road, Camberwell, Victoria 3124, Australia (a division of Pearson
Australia Group Pty Ltd); Penguin Books India Pvt Ltd, 11 Community Centre,
Panchsheel Park, New Delhi—110 017, India; Penguin Group (NZ), 67 Apollo Drive,
Rosedale, North Shore 0632, New Zealand (a division of Pearson New Zealand
Ltd); Penguin Books (South Africa) (Pty) Ltd, 24 Sturdee Avenue, Rosebank,
Johannesburg 2196, South Africa

Penguin Books Ltd, Registered Offices: 80 Strand, London WC2R 0RL, England

Published by Gotham Books, a member of Penguin Group (USA) Inc.

First printing, August 2008
10 9 8 7 6 5 4 3 2 1

Gotham Books and the skyscraper logo are trademarks of Penguin Group (USA) Inc.

LIBRARY OF CONGRESS CATALOGING-IN-PUBLICATION DATA
Barack Obama is your new bicycle : 366 ways he really cares /
Mathew Honan.— 1st ed.
   p. cm.
ISBN 978-1-59240-416-2 (pbk)
1. Obama, Barack—Humor. I. Title.
PN6231.022H66 2008
973.93102´07—dc22
                        2008019680

Printed in the United States of America
Set in various fun typefaces • Designed by Sabrina Bowers

For Harper Honan.
You are and always will be
MY NEW BICYCLE.

Acknowledgments

Thanks to Ava Honan, Terry Honan, Harper Honan, Andre Torrez, Bernardo Leigh, Conor Bezane, Daniel Dumas, David Kerns, Denise and Jason Tanz, Jeff Saunders, Joe Brown, Rob Poynter, Steve Strang, and Trica Watters for the ideas and suggestions and encouragement. Thank you to Ken and Becky Kurson, Nancy Miller, and especially Joy Tutela for helping me navigate the book publishing industry. To my editor, Patrick Mulligan, thank you for your patience and persistence. And Omar Lee: You rule. Barack Obama appreciates all your hard work.

This book was written entirely at Mojo Bicycle Café in San Francisco.

Introduction

All I wanted to do was make her laugh.

For weeks, my wife, Harper, had been throwing herself at the Obama campaign. She was making calls to voters all over the map and donating as much time and money to the campaign as she could afford. She was watching his speeches on YouTube. She was reading his policy papers and position statements, and taking pages of notes on each. By late January, Barack Obama had become her singular topic of conversation.

Now Harper is obsessive. Unlike me, she has an ability to not only focus on something with laser-like accuracy, but also sustain that focus for long periods of time. Prior to Barack's entrance into our lives, that focus had largely been on one thing: bicycles.

Mountain bikes, road bikes, track bikes, trick bikes,

time trial bikes, fixes. There is a place in Harper's heart
for them all. Our little apartment in San Francisco's Haight
district, with its views of Golden Gate, Alamo Square, and
Buena Vista Park, is a paradise of Allen wrenches, spare
tires, and chain lubricants. We are perpetually elbow-
deep in oily rags and chamois cream. And while friends
typically assume, when they see our repair stand set up
in the kitchen, that it is my doing, it is Harper who has
largely turned our lives and apartment into a bike shop.
But as we approached Valentine's Day, and the primary
season was at its most heated, I heard less and less about
bicycles, and more and more about a certain someone
named Barack.

"Barack Obama is your new bicycle."

The first time I said it was in our kitchen. It followed,
I assume, yet another ten-minute treatise on the "Urgent
Necessity of Barack Obama." She laughed. I laughed.
What I really meant, of course, was that Barack Obama
was her new obsession.

Yet in that obsession she was not alone. The entire
country was in the grip of *Obamania.* Money was pouring
into his campaign. will.i.am's video had gone completely
viral. Shepard Fairey posters were beginning to appear all
over the city. I was starting to wonder if we would soon
see his supporters carrying little red books filled with his
words of wisdom.

And so, that weekend, when I teased Harper in front of our friend Andre by again telling her that Barack Obama was her new bicycle, I was surprised to see him laugh, without having to hear the backstory. It was, I guess, obvious. Everyone loves a new bicycle, right?

Or maybe they don't. Riding home on the day before Valentine's Day on San Francisco's comprehensive, if beleaguered, public transit system, it occurred to me that barackobamaisyournewbicycle.com would be a pretty funny Web site address. Especially if it did just one thing: delivered the message that "Barack Obama is your new bicycle." But that wasn't quite it; he wasn't, for everyone, a new bicycle. Rather, he seemed to have become, over the course of those first two weeks in February, the entire country's new boyfriend.

And then all at once, the idea for the site came tumbling down to me: a single index page that fetched random phrases explaining the country's obsession with Senator Obama. (In the week following my site's launch, popular blogger Jason Kottke would dub this kind of Web site, one with just one page, a "single serving site.") I thought of a dozen or so examples before I arrived home, where I promptly registered the address, came up with another fifty or so phrases, whipped up a PHP script to serve it all, launched the site—with its large blue block Helvetica lettering—and then sent a link to it out over

Twitter, a micro-blogging platform that lets its users send quick hits out over the Internet.

I thought of it, really, as a kind of Valentine's Day present to Harper that other people might also enjoy. While traffic didn't really occur to me, I assumed I might get a hundred or so visitors over the next few days. Perhaps if I were lucky, maybe a thousand people would stop by. I added a Google traffic monitoring tool as an afterthought at Andre's suggestion.

I woke up the next morning to find the world at my in-box. Anil Dash ("The MemeMaker") had seen it and sent a link to the site out over Twitter, triggering a snowball effect. Within the first twenty-four hours, *Time, The New Republic, Politico,* and *Slate* had all linked the site, and I'd served up more than 900,000 page views. Within a week, 150,000 people had visited the site. A legion of imitator sites—all with the same Helvetica look and feel—popped up. Parody-"is your new bicycle" sites lampooned John McCain, Ron Paul, Hillary Clinton, and even Steve Jobs. Some—like "Hillary Is Mom Jeans" or "John McCain Is Your Old Jalopy"—became hits in their own right. The media came calling as well. I was interviewed by *The Washington Post* and the *Chicago Tribune.* MTV deemed me one of the "cool kids." *The New York Times* called the site "delightful." *New York* magazine put it in their "Approval Matrix." Even the European press piled on.

Everyone was full of the same questions: How many of them are there? What do they all say? How long did it take you to make it? Where did the idea come from? And, above all else: Is the site pro- or anti-Obama? Are you an Obama supporter? Or are you in Hillary's camp?

I think this ambiguity was my favorite aspect of the site, and it was completely intentional. I never meant to comment on Barack Obama, the candidate. Rather, what was interesting to me were his followers (among whom I do count myself) and his growing cult of personality. The site is an empty vessel. You bring to it your own prejudices. On any given day, I would have some reporters insist that my site was pro-Obama, and others insist it was anti-Obama. It is both. It is neither.

What it is—or at least what it is meant to be—is fun. A toy. A diversion. A snapshot of a place in time where the old guard looks poised to change and much of the nation is caught up in an electric campaign.

A campaign that, to his supporters, feels like falling in love. That feels like your very first beer. That feels like walking downstairs on Christmas morning to discover, under the tree and tied with a bow, a brand-new bicycle.

BARACK OBAMA IS YOUR NEW BICYCLE.

Barack Obama listed you as his emergency contact.

Barack Obama came across your journal on the train and mailed it back to you without reading it.

Barack Obama put a thought-provoking mix of obscure hip-hop on his Muxtape.

BARACK OBAMA KEPT THE EMBARRASSING SECRET YOU TOLD HIM WHEN YOU WERE DRUNK.

Barack Obama picked up the spare on league night.

Barack Obama let you use his hankie to blow your nose.

BARACK OBAMA
CARRIES A
PICTURE OF YOU
IN HIS WALLET.

Barack Obama bailed you out
of jail after the "pants"
incident.

Your personal reference is
Barack Obama.

Barack Obama found out your ex was going to be there and warned you ahead of time.

BARACK OBAMA DROVE YOU TO THE A.A. MEETING WHEN YOU WERE FEELING TEMPTED.

Barack Obama totally gets all your *Simpsons* references.

Barack Obama sent flowers to your office on your birthday.

Barack Obama cried upon finishing the short story that you wrote.

Barack Obama tied a fly at the end of your line.

BARACK OBAMA SANG YOU "HAPPY BIRTHDAY" ON YOUR VOICE MAIL.

Barack Obama always takes the nachos with the least cheese on them, leaving the best ones for you.

Barack Obama built you a treehouse using recycled lumber and truck tires.

BARACK OBAMA FOLDED YOU AN ORIGAMI CRANE.

Barack Obama cosigned your first auto loan.

When you came to visit, Barack Obama put a night-light in the bathroom.

Barack Obama took you out for dinner at this fantastic little hole-in-the-wall Korean BBQ joint where he's friends with the owner.

BARACK OBAMA CHANGED THE OIL IN YOUR CAR.

BARACK OBAMA HELPED YOU MOVE A SOFA.

Barack Obama volunteered to hop out and put the chains on the tires.

Barack Obama asked me to call and make sure you knew you were invited.

Barack Obama paid for the gas.

BARACK OBAMA MADE THE DINNER RESERVATIONS SIX MONTHS IN ADVANCE.

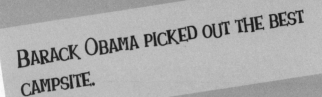

BARACK OBAMA PICKED OUT THE BEST CAMPSITE.

In the hours before a tornado blew in, BARACK OBAMA went to the hardware store and then nailed plywood over all the windows at your grandparents' home so that none of them would blow out during the storm.

Barack Obama claims your recipe for chocolate chip cookies is his favorite.

So you wouldn't get a ticket, Barack Obama dropped a quarter in the meter.

BARACK OBAMA FOUND YOUR RUNAWAY KITTY AND DECLINED THE REWARD.

Barack Obama caught a foul ball at Wrigley and handed it to you without a second thought.

BARACK OBAMA ESCORTED YOUR GRAMMA ACROSS THE STREET.

You are always in Barack Obama's "Top Eight."

Barack Obama complimented your new messenger bag.

Barack Obama scored two front-row tickets to see Arcade Fire and thought you might like to join him.

When you had a nightmare, Barack Obama sang you a lullaby.

BARACK OBAMA INSTALLED YOUR OS UPGRADE.

BARACK OBAMA BAKED YOU A PIE.

Barack Obama donated one hundred dollars to charity in your name.

Barack Obama left his Wi-Fi network open in case you wanted to use it.

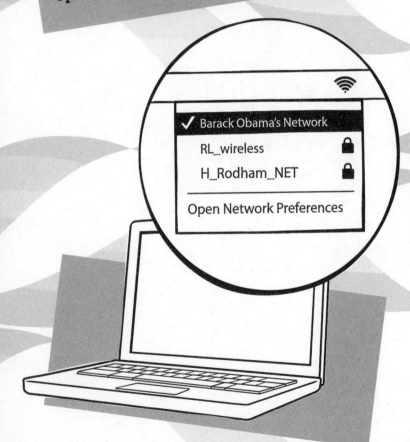

BARACK OBAMA BOUGHT YOU CANDY.

Barack Obama called your boss and raved about what great work you do.

Barack Obama gave you his entire collection of rare 1980s ska 7-inches because he heard you were into that kind of stuff and thought you might enjoy it.

Barack Obama offered you a tomato from his garden.

You and Barack Obama feel the same way about Vampire Weekend.

BARACK OBAMA PAID YOUR SPEEDING TICKET.

BARACK OBAMA SINCERELY BELIEVES YOUR DANCE MOVES ARE THE GREATEST HE'S EVER SEEN.

Barack Obama linked to your blog.

To help you save money on your power bill, Barack Obama installed solar panels on your roof.

Barack Obama composted all his table scraps for your vegetable garden.

Barack Obama sounded the alarm when he noticed smoke coming from your kitchen.

BARACK OBAMA MADE YOUR BED.

BARACK OBAMA RECORDED YOUR SHOW ON HIS MP3 PLAYER.

Barack Obama presented you with a trophy for being his "Best Friend Forever."

Barack Obama scrambled your eggs with cheese, onions, rosemary, and black pepper—just the way you like them.

Barack Obama built a birdhouse and hung it outside your window.

BARACK OBAMA MAILED YOU A VALENTINE.

Barack Obama talked you out of buying an HD DVD player last year.

BARACK OBAMA SPRAY-PAINTED YOUR OLD HOOPTIE TO LOOK LIKE A SHARK FOR BURNING MAN.

After you bonked, Barack Obama carried you across the finish line.

Barack Obama sweetened your Lapsang Souchong with the perfect amount of sugar.

Barack Obama filed your tax return for you when you were out of the country.

DESPITE HIS NERVOUSNESS WHEN CONFRONTED WITH HEIGHTS, BARACK OBAMA BUNGEE JUMPED OFF A BRIDGE WITH YOU BECAUSE HE KNEW IT WAS AN IMPORTANT MOMENT FOR THE TWO OF YOU TO SHARE.

Barack Obama saves all his quarters for the coin-op laundry in your building.

Barack Obama handed your screenplay to this producer he knows at Disney.

BARACK OBAMA LOVES YOUR LAUGH.

Barack Obama parallel parked your car in heavy traffic.

BARACK OBAMA THINKS YOU ARE CUTE.

Barack Obama rocks your band's T-shirt everywhere he goes.

Barack Obama sewed a "London Calling" patch on your denim jacket.

BARACK OBAMA WROTE AN AWESOME FRONT-PAGE POST ON METAFILTER ABOUT YOUR NEW SITE THAT GOT, LIKE, TWELVE DOZEN COMMENTS.

On the first day of spring, Barack Obama chilled out with you in Central Park all afternoon.

BARACK OBAMA LEFT A COMMENT ON YOUR BLOG.

When he saw you had some chips, Barack Obama melted some Velveeta.

Barack Obama found your
dropped a travel bug in it.

BARACK OBAMA TRANSCRIBED YOUR
NOTES SO YOU COULD GO TO THE BEACH.

Barack Obama paused the TiVo
when you went to the bathroom.

BARACK OBAMA PICKED YOU UP AT THE AIRPORT.

Barack Obama took a nap on the plane so he wouldn't be jet-lagged when he got to your house.

Barack Obama bronzed your hacky sack.

BARACK OBAMA PUSHED YOU IN THE SWINGS ON THE PLAYGROUND.

BARACK OBAMA LIVES NEXT DOOR TO YOUR MOM.

Barack Obama sold your old car on Craigslist.

Barack Obama organized your closet.

Barack Obama covered for you when you were late to a meeting.

BARACK OBAMA SAVED HIS DESSERT FOR YOU.

BARACK OBAMA TURNED YOU ON TO DAVID BOWIE'S WORK FROM THE 1970S.

Barack Obama triangulated your location and called in a rescue crew.

Barack Obama sketched you in silhouette.

Barack Obama showed up with a biscuit for your dog.

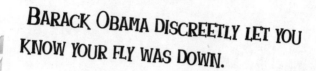

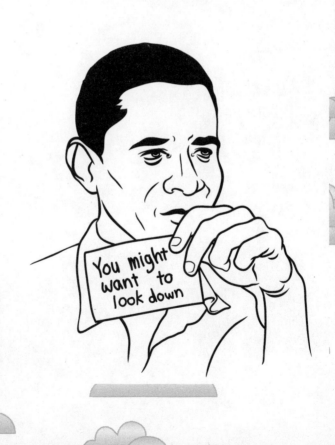

Barack Obama dropped off your late book at the library and paid the fine.

BARACK OBAMA CLEANED OUT YOUR GUTTERS.

Barack Obama came up with a three-hour jazz playlist for your cocktail party.

Barack Obama tuned your guitar.

Barack Obama was first to arrive at your premiere gallery show.

BARACK OBAMA FIXED YOUR CAR.

Barack Obama walked you out to your car in the rain.

BARACK OBAMA SHARED HIS
UMBRELLA WITH YOU.

BARACK OBAMA
BUILT YOU A
ROBOT.

Barack Obama never sends you
e-mail forwards.

Barack Obama pressure-washed the soot off of your exterior walls after your neighbor's house went up in flames.

Barack Obama checks your FriendFeed, like, ten times a day.

BARACK OBAMA ADJUSTED THE PRESSURE IN YOUR TIRES.

BARACK OBAMA SENT YOU FLOWERS.

Barack Obama debugged the source code in your Web page.

Barack Obama ordered you a gift subscription to this totally hip new magazine everyone's talking about.

BARACK OBAMA SHOWED YOU HOW TO TIE A FULL WINDSOR.

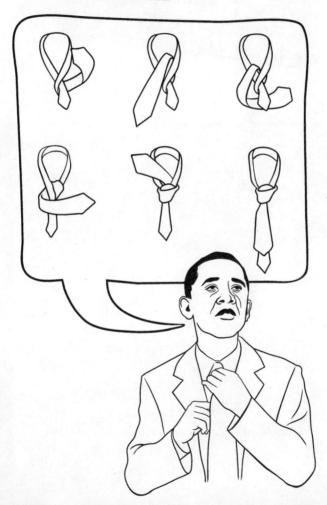

Barack Obama mowed your yard while you slept it off.

Barack Obama noticed what a pretty color your eyes are with that sweater.

Barack Obama fixed you a bowl of hot chicken soup because he thought it might make you feel a little better.

BARACK OBAMA KNOWS ALL THE WORDS TO YOUR FAVORITE SONG.

BARACK OBAMA LENT YOU HIS JACKET.

Barack Obama read your first draft and left some brilliantly constructive notes in the margins.

Barack Obama planted tulips in your window box.

Not only did he know how to do it properly, but when you began choking, BARACK OBAMA sprang into action and performed the Heimlich maneuver on you without hesitation.

BARACK OBAMA PLAYED HOPSCOTCH WITH YOUR COUSIN.

Barack Obama poured your latte so the foam made a little picture of a bird.

Barack Obama sprang for your lunch.

Barack Obama helped you find an apartment.

Barack Obama found your car keys.

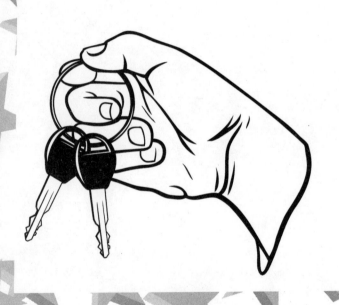

Barack Obama crammed all night for the SAT with you.

Barack Obama let you wear his favorite T-shirt.

BARACK OBAMA WASHED THE WINDOWS WHEN YOU STOPPED FOR GAS.

BARACK OBAMA DEDICATED A SONG TO YOU.

Barack Obama listens to your Last.fm channel every single day.

Barack Obama steam-cleaned your carpets.

BARACK OBAMA MADE YOU A MIXTAPE.

Songs
for You

Barack it 2 U

Barack Obama left a message with your mom to let her know you were okay.

Barack Obama designed the template for your blog.

Barack Obama mixed you a mean sazerac with real absinthe.

BARACK OBAMA SET YOUR VOICE AS HIS RINGTONE.

BARACK OBAMA PATCHED THE HOLE WHERE YOU TORE YOUR JEANS.

While you were in the shower, Barack Obama toasted a bagel for you.

Barack Obama swept up all the glass after you dropped your soda.

BARACK OBAMA CARRIED YOUR BOOKBAG.

Barack Obama texted you to let you know where the party is.

BARACK OBAMA SHOWED YOU A
SHORTCUT HOME.

Barack Obama batted in the winning
run for your softball team.

Barack Obama left a really generous
tip at your table.

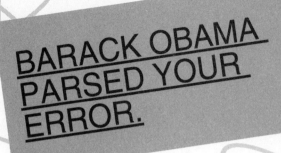

BARACK OBAMA PARSED YOUR ERROR.

Barack Obama stopped to pet your dog when he saw it leashed outside the café.

Barack Obama taught you how to do a totes impressive card trick.

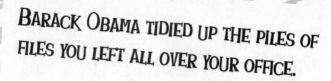

BARACK OBAMA TIDIED UP THE PILES OF FILES YOU LEFT ALL OVER YOUR OFFICE.

Barack Obama brought back a cheese-and-tomato sandwich when you were stuck at your desk.

Barack Obama took your mother shoe-shopping at Barneys.

BARACK OBAMA RAN OUT TO PICK UP A COUPLE OF PIZZAS BEFORE THE GAME STARTS.

Barack Obama unlocked your iPhone.

BARACK OBAMA OFFERED YOU HIS SEAT.

Barack Obama took you to the state fair and bought you funnel cake.

Barack Obama convinced you that a neck tattoo might not be such a good idea.

EVEN THOUGH IT'S KIND OF A PAIN, BARACK OBAMA BRINGS HIS OWN MUG TO THE COFFEE SHOP BECAUSE YOU TOLD HIM IT WAS BETTER FOR THE EARTH.

Barack Obama plugged the leak in your radiator.

BARACK OBAMA WANTED YOU TO HAVE SOME CUPCAKES.

Barack Obama shoveled the snow from your walkway.

BARACK OBAMA LENT YOU HIS FAVORITE BOOK.

Barack Obama washed and dried the dishes after the party wound down.

Barack Obama correctly diagnosed your symptoms.

BARACK OBAMA DROVE YOU TO THE EMERGENCY ROOM AFTER YOUR ILL-FATED SOCCER GAME.

Barack Obama gave up his place in line so he could sit with you.

BARACK OBAMA FAVORITED YOUR PHOTO.

Barack Obama explained the DVD-extra ending of I Am Legend to you.

Barack Obama signed for your package while you were out.

Barack Obama gave you some all-natural biodegradable hand soap scented with a hint of organic cedar oil.

BARACK OBAMA CLEANED HIS PLATE WHEN HE HAD DINNER AT YOUR AUNTIE'S HOUSE.

Barack Obama said he'd like to drive so you could take a nap.

Barack Obama changed out your kitty litter for you.

Barack Obama let you have his taxi.

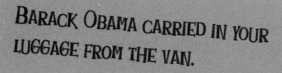

Barack Obama carried in your luggage from the van.

Barack Obama mashed up two of your favorite songs.

You don't have to worry about bullies, because Barack Obama is protecting you.

Barack Obama installed a new alarm system in your car so it would quit going off in the middle of the night.

BARACK OBAMA INVITED YOU TO HIS THANKSGIVING DINNER.

Barack Obama let you win at Scrabulous.

Barack Obama showed you how to get more "star power" on Guitar Hero.

Barack Obama wrote your name in calligraphy.

BARACK OBAMA SPRAYED THE WASP NEST IN YOUR EAVES BECAUSE HE KNEW YOU WERE ALLERGIC.

BARACK OBAMA ADDED YOU AS A FRIEND.

Barack Obama has added you as a friend!

If you accept this invitation, Barack wil be added to your contacts list.

Accept   Decline

Barack Obama composed a song in honor of your birthday.

BARACK OBAMA SMILED WHEN HE HEARD ME MENTION YOUR NAME.

Barack Obama references you in all his conversations.

Barack Obama told a story about the time you went camping together.

BARACK OBAMA TRANSLATED FOR YOU WHEN YOU WENT SURFING TOGETHER IN BAJA.

Barack Obama let you use his calling card.

BARACK OBAMA SUBSCRIBED TO YOUR FEED.

Barack Obama lent you his BlackBerry so you could send an e-mail.

Barack Obama rented a ladder so he could wash the skylights on your roof.

Barack Obama stored your kayak in his garage.

BARACK OBAMA CAME TO VISIT YOUR DAD WHEN HE WAS IN THE HOSPITAL.

Barack Obama handed you the keys to his lake cabin and said to use it whenever you'd like.

Barack Obama taught you how to snowboard.

Barack Obama woke up early to wish you luck before the race.

BARACK OBAMA BOOKMARKED YOUR WEB SITE.

BARACK OBAMA POURED YOU A CUP OF COFFEE.

Barack Obama commissioned his favorite artist to paint your portrait.

Don't worry about that red-wine stain on your sweater; Barack Obama knows how to get it out.

BARACK OBAMA DONATED HIS TIME TO YOUR FUND-RAISER.

BARACK OBAMA WARMED YOUR CAR UP FOR YOU.

Barack Obama wanted to make sure you're comfortable.

Barack Obama pulled over so you could pee.

Barack Obama checked under your bed for monsters.

BARACK OBAMA INCLUDED YOU IN THE MURAL HE PAINTED AT THE COMMUNITY CENTER.

Barack Obama offered to be the designated driver.

Barack Obama let you crash on his couch.

BARACK OBAMA THOUGHT YOU COULD USE SOME CHOCOLATE.

Barack Obama installed a dimmer switch in your living room.

BARACK OBAMA TIVO'D "HEROES" FOR YOU.

Barack Obama held your hair when you were sick.

Barack Obama rode the old wooden coaster at the Santa Cruz Boardwalk with you.

Barack Obama cleared out your cache.

BARACK OBAMA PRONOUNCED YOUR NAME CORRECTLY.

When he heard you were confused, **BARACK OBAMA** patiently spent, like, a half hour or so catching you up on *Lost* and explaining his time-travel theory about the island.

Barack Obama opened your beer bottle with his lighter.

Barack Obama saved you a seat on the N Judah.

BARACK OBAMA CREATED A WIKIPEDIA ENTRY ABOUT YOU.

Barack Obama paid for the first round.

Barack Obama held the rod while you hung your drapes.

Barack Obama came running when you called his name in the night.

BARACK OBAMA ALWAYS PICKS UP WHEN HE SEES YOUR NAME ON HIS CALLER ID.

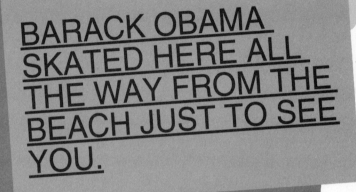

BARACK OBAMA SKATED HERE ALL THE WAY FROM THE BEACH JUST TO SEE YOU.

Barack Obama has your back in any fight.

Barack Obama really digs your new haircut.

Barack Obama beta tested your new Web app.

BARACK OBAMA PLANTED A TREE TO COMMEMORATE YOUR ANNIVERSARY.

BARACK OBAMA FOLLOWED YOU ON TWITTER.

Barack Obama mailed you a "get well soon" card.

Barack Obama joined your book club and showed up prepared.

BARACK OBAMA RECITED A POEM THAT REMINDED HIM OF YOU.

Barack Obama learned all the other parts just so you could rehearse your role.

EVEN THOUGH IT WAS THE MIDDLE OF THE NIGHT, WHEN BARACK OBAMA HEARD YOU WERE OUT OF GAS, HE DRAGGED HIMSELF OUT OF BED AND DROVE OUT INTO THE COUNTRY TO BRING YOU A JERRICAN FULL OF FUEL.

Barack Obama set up a monthly budget for you.

Barack Obama created a spreadsheet to track your expenses.

Barack Obama climbed Kilimanjaro and wrote your name in the logbook.

BARACK OBAMA RUBBED SUNSCREEN ONTO YOUR SHOULDERS SO YOU WOULDN'T BURN.

<u>BARACK OBAMA SPENT THE AFTERNOON SETTING UP YOUR ROUTER.</u>

Barack Obama finds your ratty old Adidas endearing.

Barack Obama recycled all your old bottles and cans.

BARACK OBAMA GROOMED YOUR ILL-TEMPERED CAT.

Barack Obama took the red-eye so he could see you right away.

BARACK OBAMA DREW YOUR PICTURE IN THE SAND.

Barack Obama carried your groceries up four flights of stairs.

Barack Obama untangled your hair after you spent all afternoon in the ocean.

BARACK OBAMA GAVE YOU A KNOWING GLANCE.

Barack Obama blazed a trail through the brush for you to follow.

Barack Obama sailed all the way around the isthmus to come visit you.

Barack Obama paddled all the way around the pond to bring you hot dogs.

Barack Obama buttoned up your coat so you wouldn't have to take your hands out of your mittens.

BARACK OBAMA HELD YOUR HAND WHEN YOU WERE FRIGHTENED.

While you were traveling in Spain, Barack Obama renovated your hardwood floors.

BARACK OBAMA PAINTED A DOZEN EASTER EGGS FOR YOUR NIECE'S PARTY.

Barack Obama tossed you a rope when you fell out of the raft.

Barack Obama polished all the silverware before your dinner party.

Barack Obama understood when you flaked out on him.

Barack Obama waited for you at the top of the hill.

BARACK OBAMA REMEMBERED YOUR BIRTHDAY.

Barack Obama pretended not to notice when you farted in his car.

Barack Obama wrote a glowing letter of reference for you when you applied for a job.

Barack Obama thought to say "God bless you" after you sneezed.

BARACK OBAMA SCRUBBED THE GRAFFITI OFF THE FRONT OF YOUR BUILDING.

During your convalescence, while recovering from a horrid case of the shingles, BARACK OBAMA swung by with a care package of all the latest magazines, plus a few books and some DVDs to keep you entertained.

Barack Obama wore a yellow ribbon in honor of your neighbor serving in Iraq.

Barack Obama adjusted the EQ on your stereo and fixed all the levels.

Barack Obama spotted you on the bench press.

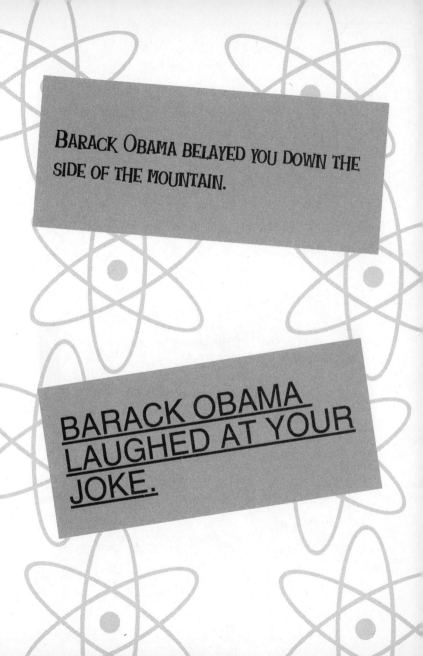

BARACK OBAMA BELAYED YOU DOWN THE SIDE OF THE MOUNTAIN.

BARACK OBAMA LAUGHED AT YOUR JOKE.

Barack Obama arranged flowers in a vase and left them on your doorstep.

Barack Obama filtered out the spam from your inbox.

Barack Obama screenprinted your design on his T-shirt.

BARACK OBAMA SHAVED HIS HEAD SO YOU WOULDN'T HAVE TO DO IT ALONE.

BARACK OBAMA RELATES TO WHAT YOU ARE SAYING.

Barack Obama waited on hold for a half hour with Apple tech support to get your MacBook fixed.

Barack Obama changed your nephew's diaper because he knew it grossed you out.

Barack Obama deposited some money in your account to keep your check from bouncing.

BARACK OBAMA CAME TO SEE YOUR PLAY.

So you wouldn't be late, BARACK OBAMA set your clock ahead for DAYLIGHT SAVING TIME.

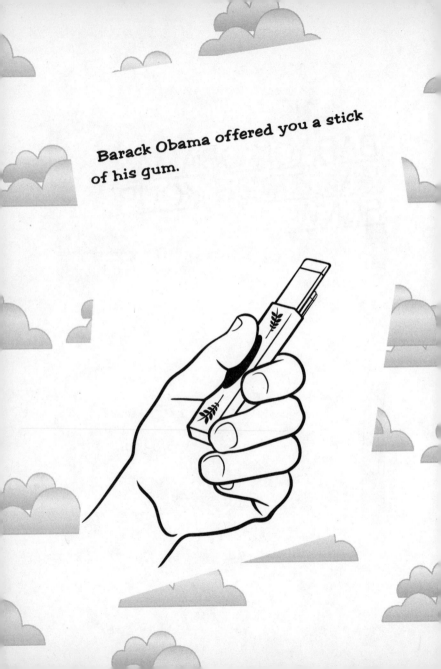

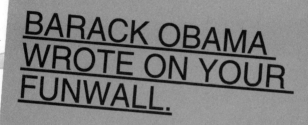

BARACK OBAMA WROTE ON YOUR FUNWALL.

Barack Obama genuinely wants to know how your day went.

BARACK OBAMA BABYSAT FOR YOU AT THE LAST MINUTE BECAUSE HE KNEW YOU REALLY NEEDED A NIGHT OUT.

Barack Obama knows about this great new Thai place he thinks you'll dig.

Barack Obama waded into the stream and plucked your sunglasses from the icy depths.

Barack Obama slid over in the backseat so you wouldn't have to walk around.

BARACK OBAMA E-MAILED YOUR DAD AND TOLD HIM HOW GREAT YOU ARE.

Barack Obama chaperoned your middle school dance.

BARACK OBAMA RESPECTS YOUR OPINION.

Barack Obama grew you a garden of jasmine and succulents.

BARACK OBAMA RETILED YOUR KITCHEN FLOOR IN A MOSAIC PATTERN.

On the wall along his staircase, Barack Obama hung your picture alongside those of his family.

Barack Obama danced with your mom at your sister's wedding.

BARACK OBAMA IS CHRISTMAS MORNING.

Barack Obama frosted your cake so it looks like R2-D2.

Barack Obama learned Italian so he could translate for you at the opera.

BARACK OBAMA IS REMINDED OF YOU WHEN HE DREAMS OF A BETTER NATION.

Barack Obama stitched your name into the sleeve of his hoodie.

BARACK OBAMA SAID HE REALLY WANTED TO MEET YOU.

Barack Obama made you a few different sandwiches to take with you on the flight.

Barack Obama gathered firewood so you'd stay warm all night.

BARACK OBAMA GRILLED YOUR STEAK JUST THE WAY YOU LIKE IT.

Barack Obama mailed you a postcard from his vacation.

Barack Obama invited you into his skybox for the play-offs.

Barack Obama LOL'd at the link you sent him.

Barack Obama set your picture as his avatar.

Barack Obama bookmarked your Tumblr page.

BARACK OBAMA WROTE A LETTER TO THE EDITOR ENDORSING YOUR AWESOMENESS.

Barack Obama subscribed to your channel on YouTube.

BARACK OBAMA IS FRESH-BAKED BREAD.

Barack Obama bunted you over to third.

Barack Obama delivered your firstborn in the back of a taxicab.

WHEN ONE OF YOUR VOCALISTS CAME DOWN WITH A NASTY BRONCHITIS BUG, BARACK OBAMA SANG BACKUP IN YOUR BAND.

BARACK OBAMA IS THAT NEW-CAR SMELL.

Barack Obama added you to his
Buddy List.

Barack Obama lifted you up out of the
mud when you wiped out.

Barack Obama held the door on the
subway for you.

BARACK OBAMA WALKED ACROSS THE WILLIAMSBURG BRIDGE TO COME MEET YOUR FRIENDS.

Barack Obama double-dated with you at prom.

Barack Obama rehearsed with you all night long before your big audition.

Barack Obama started a tab.

BARACK OBAMA IS A LAZY SUMMER AFTERNOON.

Barack Obama taught you how to ollie.

Barack Obama crocheted a line from a song that you love into an afghan and gave it to you for your birthday.

Barack Obama hiked over the pass to help you earn your merit badge.

Barack Obama commissioned an art student to paint your portrait in his breakfast nook so he could see you every morning.

BARACK OBAMA BREWED YOU A CUP OF TEA.

Barack Obama surrounds himself with little reminders of the time you traveled together in India.

For Roskilde last summer, Barack Obama flew to Denmark to come meet you.

Barack Obama scaled the fence to get your Frisbee out of the neighbor's yard.

BARACK OBAMA IS YOUR TRUSTY FRENCH BULLDOG.

Barack Obama introduced you to Bob Dylan after the show.

Barack Obama never talks like Austin Powers because he knows it annoys you.

BARACK OBAMA IS THE FIRST REAL SNOW OF THE SEASON.

Barack Obama lent you his El Camino to move your dresser.

Barack Obama ordered a Nonfat Macchiato for you.

Barack Obama shelled an enormous bagful of peas for your picnic.

Barack Obama scared the bear away from your campsite.

BARACK OBAMA SPENT HIS WHOLE SATURDAY IN DETENTION JUST TO HANG OUT WITH YOU.

BARACK OBAMA IS YOUR FIRST CUP OF COFFEE.

Barack Obama donated a kidney to your little brother.

BARACK OBAMA VOTED "THIS IS GOOD" ON YOUR FILE.

Even though it was sort of embarrassing, Barack Obama took your little Chihuahua to the dog park when you were out of town and cleaned up his wee little poo in wee little biodegradable Baggies.

Barack Obama swam across the channel with you.

Barack Obama roller-skated backward at your party.

YOU REMIND BARACK OBAMA OF THE FRESH MOUNTAIN MORNING AIR.

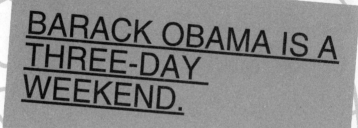

BARACK OBAMA IS A THREE-DAY WEEKEND.

Barack Obama hung the sheets out on a line to dry before your visit.

Barack Obama backed up all your important data to an external hard drive before your server crashed.

Barack Obama put together a team of investors to produce your documentary.

BARACK OBAMA IS A ROSE GARDEN.

BARACK OBAMA JUMPED YOUR BATTERY AT SIX A.M. AFTER YOU LEFT THE LIGHTS ON ALL NIGHT.

Barack Obama carved the turkey at your Christmas get-together.

Barack Obama printed five hundred copies of your zine and sold them all over campus.

Barack Obama used rocks to spell your name in Morse code in his xeriscape garden.

Barack Obama blurbed your book with a glowing review.

BARACK OBAMA CAUGHT YOUR BABY WHEN SHE SLIPPED THROUGH YOUR ARMS.

BARACK OBAMA IS YOUR RECORD COLLECTION.

Barack Obama validated your HTML.

BARACK OBAMA IS YOUR NEW SMARTPHONE.

Barack Obama trained your dog to fetch you a PBR from the fridge.

Barack Obama pitched a no-hitter in your league's play-offs.

Barack Obama rebuilt the engine on your motorbike.

Barack Obama gave you the first bite of his jelly roll.

BARACK OBAMA IS YOUR NEXT VACATION.

Barack Obama reminded you to floss.

BARACK OBAMA COVERED FOR YOU
WHEN YOU PLAYED HOOKY FROM WORK.

BARACK OBAMA IS
YOUR VINTAGE
VESPA.

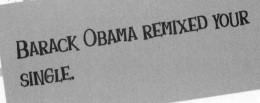

BARACK OBAMA REMIXED YOUR SINGLE.

Barack Obama paid your fare at the tollbooth.

Barack Obama carpooled to work with your uncle.

After correctly filling out your NCAA tournament bracket for your office's March Madness pool, BARACK OBAMA refused to take a dime of the winnings even though you had to be forcibly talked out of slotting the Blue Devils as tournament champs and, had it not been for his advice, you would have chosen Duke to go all the way like everyone else.

Barack Obama trued your wheelset.

Barack Obama suggested a great dentist.

BARACK OBAMA PERCOLATED A POT OF
COFFEE AND POURED SOME IN A THERMOS
FOR YOU TO TAKE TO WORK.

Barack Obama sealed your photograph in a time capsule he buried at the schoolyard.

Barack Obama kissed the boo-boo on your knee and made the pain go away.

Barack Obama meditated on your problem until he came up with a solution.

BARACK OBAMA WORE HIS VINTAGE SMITHS T-SHIRT TO YOUR PARTY BECAUSE HE KNEW YOU'D APPRECIATE IT.

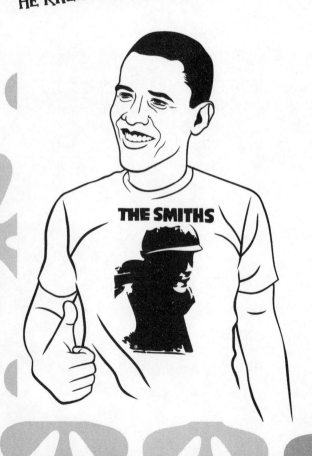

Barack Obama totally understands when you need some time alone.

Barack Obama stopped shopping at his favorite store because they were rude to you.

Barack Obama coached you every night for weeks before your *Jeopardy!* appearance.

BARACK OBAMA IS THE BEGINNING OF SPRING TRAINING.

BARACK OBAMA LISTENS TO YOUR PODCAST AS SOON AS IT SHOWS UP IN iTUNES.

Barack Obama recognized you from afar.

Even though he was totally busy (and not a nerd), Barack Obama went with you to Comic-Con.

Barack Obama built a fire to warm the cabin before you got up.

Barack Obama Photoshopped the blemishes out of your picture—not because he thought you needed the touch-up, but, rather, because he knew you were self-conscious about them.

BARACK OBAMA COVERED ONE OF YOUR SONGS ON HIS NEW ALBUM.

Barack Obama wove you a friendship bracelet on the last day of camp.

BARACK OBAMA GAVE YOU A PUPPY.

Barack Obama explored the caves behind Old Man Wilkins' barn with you.

Barack Obama snuck out of the house to go with you to the concert in the city.

Barack Obama dugg your link.

BARACK OBAMA WAIVED HIS FINDER'S FEE BECAUSE HE WAS JUST HAPPY YOU JOINED.

Barack Obama paid right up when you won the bet.

Barack Obama watered your garden.

Barack Obama jumped out of a plane for your going-away party.

BARACK OBAMA ACCOMPANIED YOU ON A WINE-TASTING TRIP TO NAPA.

Barack Obama argued your case pro bono.

Barack Obama encouraged you to follow your dream of becoming the greatest Parkour traceur in all of North America.

Barack Obama shifted his weight so your leg wouldn't fall asleep.

Barack Obama took the middle seat so you could have the aisle.

BARACK OBAMA SMOKED A TURKEY BREAST BEFORE YOUR GARDEN PARTY.

Barack Obama cut his hair just like yours.

Barack Obama oiled your hinges.

Barack Obama sharpened all your kitchen knives.

BARACK OBAMA FILLETED YOUR CATCH.

Barack Obama congratulated you after a hard-fought game of Ping-Pong.

Barack Obama recorded the outgoing message on your answering machine.

Barack Obama adjusted the clock on your parents' DVD player.

BARACK OBAMA SCULPTED YOUR IMAGE IN CLAY.

Barack Obama shouted your name from the top of Half Dome.

Barack Obama cried, unabashedly, with you at the movies.

Barack Obama climbed up the wall and into an open window so you wouldn't have to call a locksmith.

BARACK OBAMA CALLED YOUR MOM ON MOTHER'S DAY JUST TO SAY HI.

Barack Obama counted all your pennies and rolled them up in paper.

Barack Obama mapped out a new dungeon and rolled up a totally badass paladin for your first game of D&D.

Barack Obama swears nobody else can tell a joke as well as you can.

BARACK OBAMA SPRINTED TO THE CORNER STORE FOR SOME OJ WHEN YOUR BLOOD SUGAR WAS LOW.

When your back hurt, Barack Obama walked on it until he worked out all the kinks.

Barack Obama stuck by your side throughout the trial because he knew you were innocent.

Barack Obama brought along an extra baguette for you in his messenger bag in case you wanted a snack.

BARACK OBAMA SUCKED ALL THE POISON OUT OF YOUR SNAKEBITE.

Barack Obama sanded down the rough edges because he knows you have soft hands and he didn't want you to get a splinter.

Barack Obama swapped all your incandescents for compact fluorescents.

Barack Obama did the dishes so you could chill after dinner.

BARACK OBAMA BEDAZZLED YOUR CELL PHONE.

Your new flat-screen TV?
Wall-mounted by Barack Obama.

Barack Obama designed a save-the-date mailer for your wedding.

Barack Obama transferred his frequent-flier miles over to you so you could take that trip to Maui you were always talking about.

BARACK OBAMA BURNED SAGE IN YOUR APARTMENT AFTER A ROUGH BREAKUP.

Barack Obama called the radio station and dedicated a song to you.

Barack Obama abandoned his quest for the summit to carry you down.

Barack Obama made a heartfelt toast at your wedding.

BARACK OBAMA SCUFFED UP YOUR CHUCK TAYLORS SO THEY WOULDN'T LOOK SO DORKY.

Barack Obama selected the perfect Sangiovese to go with your dinner.

Barack Obama sold your niece's Girl Scout Cookies at his office.

Barack Obama followed your directions even though he was pretty sure his way was faster

WHILE ON VACATION IN CENTRAL AMERICA, BARACK OBAMA DISCOVERED AN ENTIRELY NEW SPECIES OF ORCHID AND NAMED IT AFTER YOU.

Barack Obama
autographed
your book.